THE WILD UNKNOWN JOURNAL

THE WILD UNKNOWN
JOURNAL

KIM KRANS

HarperOne
An Imprint of HarperCollinsPublishers

HarperOne

HarperCollins books may be purchased for educational, business, or sales promotional use. For information, please email the Special Markets Department at SPsales@harpercollins.com.

HarperCollins website: http://www.harpercollins.com

FIRST EDITION

Designed by Kim Krans & Su Barber

Library of Congress Cataloging-in-Publication Data is available upon request.
Name: Krans, Kim, author
Title: The Wild Unknown Journal / Kim Krans
Description: San Francisco, CA : HarperOne, [2018]:
Krans, Kim, author

ISBN 978-0-06-287137-4

18 19 20 21 22 LSC 10 9 8 7 6 5 4 3 2 1

for Ms. Parsons
MY FIRST DRAWING TEACHER

CONTENTS

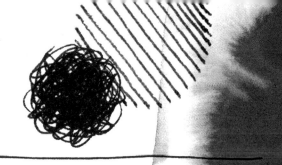

welcome

WILD UNKNOWN

you have

THE LABYRINTH

8

to the

JOURNAL

now entered

OF CREATIVITY

WHAT IS A LABYRINTH?

WITHIN
THE WALLS
OF THE LABYRINTH YOU
WILL FIND NO DIRECT PATH AND
NO RIGHT ANSWERS. IN EVERY WAY, THE
LABYRINTH MIMICS THE CREATIVE PROCESS. NO
MATTER WHAT ANYONE SAYS, THERE IS NO UNIVERSAL
MAP. THE WAY CANNOT BE KNOWN, BUT MUST BE
TRAVELED. IT IS DIFFICULT, BUT BEYOND REWARDING.
THE LABYRINTH PULLS YOU TOWARD ITS CENTER
WHERE FOR A MOMENT YOU GLIMPSE THE INFINITE
MAGIC OF THE CREATIVE SELF. CAN WE REACH THE
CENTER? I CAN'T PRETEND TO KNOW FOR CERTAIN. MY
INSTINCT IS TO SAY WE ONLY GLIMPSE IT FOR BRIEF
MOMENTS. WHY? BECAUSE WITHIN THE CENTER OF THE
LABYRINTH YOU WILL FIND ANOTHER, DEEPER, MORE
COMPLEX AND MAGICAL LABYRINTH. THIS GOES ON AND
ON INFINITELY. THANKFULLY THERE IS NO PERFECT. IF
THERE WERE, THAT WOULD BE THE END. CREATIVITY
BY ITS VERY NATURE HAS NO FINALITY, ONLY
GROWTH. LET YOURSELF BE PULLED
TOWARD THE CENTER.
I WILL MEET YOU
THERE.

WHAT IS SEEKING YOU?

YOU DO
NOT HAVE TO GO THE
WHOLE WAY ON YOUR OWN. YOU
ONLY HAVE TO TAKE THE FIRST STEP.
"IT" WILL MEET YOU ALONG THE WAY, AND YOU
WILL RECOGNIZE EACH OTHER, LIKE OLD FRIENDS.
WHAT IS "IT" YOU ASK? "IT" IS THE CENTER OF THE
LABYRINTH, WHICH SOME MAY CALL THE SELF, THE
SPIRIT, THE SOUL, THE GREAT MYSTERY, THE ABYSS. IT
RESPONDS TO MANY NAMES. IT IS AN UNKNOWN FORCE
THAT IS ALWAYS, IN ALL WAYS, REACHING OUT TO US. WHEN
WE CONNECT TO IT, THROUGH CREATIVE PRACTICE OR
ANY OTHER MEANS, IT WELCOMES US ONTO ITS BACK. IT
CARRIES US THROUGH THE LABYRINTH OF LIFE LIKE
A CHARIOT GALLOPING TOWARD THE LIGHT. WE MAY
THINK WE KNOW WHAT WE WANT, WHAT WE
NEED, AND WHERE WE ARE GOING, BUT THE
CHARIOT CARRIES US SOMEWHERE NEW.
THIS JOURNEY IS THE ESSENCE
OF THE CREATIVE
LIFE.

CREATIVE

There is a wondrous word that is used consistently in my three favorite disciplines (spirituality, psychology, and creativity). This word is PRACTICE. **BUT WHAT DOES IT REALLY MEAN?** When are we practicing and when are we doing "the real thing"? This is an unanswerable question. One could easily argue practice never ends. One could also argue that every moment is the real thing. So my humble answer to the question is: Both. Always. Let's envision a professional athlete. When they are training, they are surely practicing. Yet when they enter a competition, they are also practicing "the real thing." This is slippery territory... but stay with me. The slipperiness comes because "the real thing" is elusive. It moves ahead as we grow. Like the center of the labyrinth, it pulls us deeper as we approach it, leading us into new territory. When the athlete looks back at the competition years later, they will realize it was only practice, leading them to the present moment. There are signifiers, though, that tell us when we are practicing.

WHEN WE PRACTICE, WE ARE PRESENT.

When we practice, we are in a headspace of humility, expansion, and a desire to learn. It might even be so engaging (and fun) that we lose track of time. This is the headspace I have chased my whole life. In fact, I am practicing writing **AT THIS VERY MOMENT.** Through language I am attempting to be present with you amid the goings-on in my life. When we practice, we show up. It happens every time **LIKE MAGIC.** As for my own personal practice, I have been drawing nearly every day since I was fifteen. I was lucky to have a drawing teacher with a disciplined

PRACTICE

approach to draftsmanship. She instilled in me the idea that if I drew and drew and drew, that eventually the line would awaken and come to life, that my **DRAWINGS COULD CONTAIN PSYCHIC ENERGY** that others could feel. This idea compelled me. It led me to draw like a maniac all through my teens and twenties. Perhaps the line did awaken at some point. Perhaps you can feel all those hours spent calling the force forward. No matter what your relationship to creativity or spirituality is, my hope is that you use this journal to reconnect to the idea of practice. To YOUR PRACTICE, **WHATEVER THAT LOOKS LIKE.** It could be writing, meditating, sketching, dancing, drawing, or just playing around with line and color. Creativity will remain an elusive gem until we call it toward us with consistency and longing. Then... at some point you will notice the practice pulling you toward "the real thing." And what is "the real thing," you dare to ask? We've all felt it and seen it before. When you witness any creative force— the stroke of a painter, the last line of a poem, the baker's bread in your mouth, the snowboarder spinning through the sky—you are witnessing first-hand the sum of all their practice pitched perfectly with the grace of letting go. The two are the forever dueling forces of life, of creativity. They are **THE RIDER AND THE CHARIOT** together at last. For a moment, all is right in the world, and we sense ourselves at the very center of life's labyrinth. May you use these pages to **REACH OUT TO THAT INFINITE FORCE WITHIN** again and again and again.

PRACTICE MAKES PRACTICE

WISDOM FROM THE SAGE PATANJALI:

any practice done consistently over a long period of time with love in your heart produces results. any practice done consistently over a long period of time with love in your heart produces results. any practice done consistently over a long period of time with love in your heart produces results. any practice done consistently over a long period of time with love in your heart produces results. any practice done consistently over a long period of time with love in your heart produces results. any practice done consistently over a long period of time with love in your heart produces results. any practice done consistently over a long period of time with love in your heart produces results. any practice done consistently over a long period of time with love in your heart produces results. any practice done consistently over a long period of time with love in your heart produces results.

YOU & I ARE
collaborators
TRAVERSING
space
—AND—
time

You and I have not met, yet within the magical pages of this journal we become collaborators. This is an intimate experience. I have added a bit of myself, my thinking, my dreams, and my creativity to every page. You will do the same. We will do the best we can together. Right now I am going through a certain time in my life that is full of mysterious feelings and junctures. It's likely you are too. No matter if you are at a high point or a low point, are elated or confused, whether you use this book in 2018, 2020, or 2100... you and I will still be building a unique collaborative image on every page. Creativity supersedes time and place. If you don't believe me, just take the drawing of the crystal on the opposite page. It is the gem that hangs in the window of my studio by the Oregon Coast on this sunny day in February. I have brought this crystal into your hands, delivered the image to you at this very moment. How can this be? Where was it before? It was with me, wasn't it? Now we share it. Now it is your turn... to color it, disguise it, add a rainbow, lightning, collage an eagle into the center, write a poem across its shape, perhaps paint hands that reach toward its light. What you do with it will be unique, never to be repeated, a joining of your psyche and mine. Did you ever think we would make art together? In the labyrinth, anything is possible. We have traversed space and time together, you and I. This is the magic of creativity and collaboration. Go ahead and feel it.

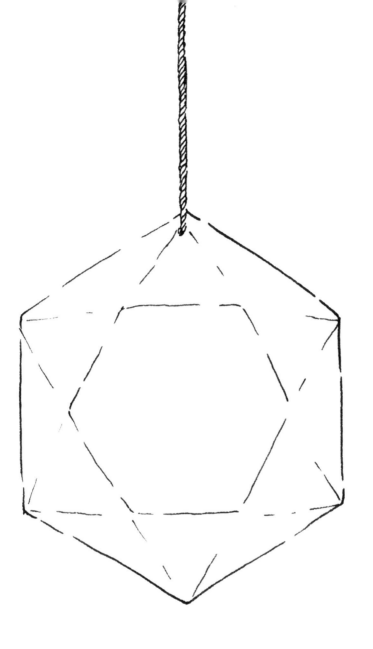

I would especially like if you show the world this special moment you and I have shared!
What does our crystal collaboration look like? #twujournal

THERE THERE
IS IS
NO ONLY
RIGHT ACTION
OR OR
WRONG INACTION

HOW TO USE
THIS JOURNAL

←——— What does this mean? It means that the only wrong way to use this journal is to not use it at all, to not explore the pages that stir curiosity in you. That is the whole idea... to summon your sense of wonder, to challenge you, to provide a space for the wild and the unknown within you to be expressed.

Once you get started, you may find that it seems like there is a "correct" way to respond to certain pages. I'm playing a bit of a trickster here though (oh, how the artist loves to play tricks!) so please take my prompts as literally or as metaphorically as you want to. For example, let's look at the "extend" prompt. On the next page you'll find four ways you could approach it. Each is valid, "correct," expansive, and wondrous. There are a million more responses I could envision, and a zillion more I can't envision at this moment but would love for you to show me on social media or elsewhere. How many responses can come from the prompt "extend"? It's up to you to decide... these are just a few ———→

POSSIBILITY ONE

EXTEND

POSSIBILITY TWO

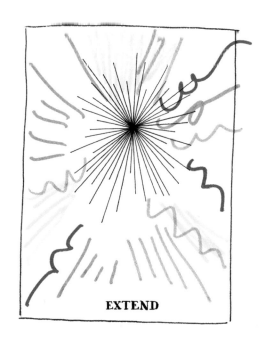

EXTEND

YOU THINK: Well I'll just extend the lines! This is the obvious solution! I SAY: Yes! You will train your eye and hand to work together, to draw those straight lines without getting too fussy — this is no small feat. You will end up with an energetic, expressive page. Do it!

YOU THINK: what does "extend" really mean? Hmmmm... I will extend the lines visually and energetically, but not with the same line. I'll do it with paint, with color! I SAY: Yes! Here we go, my friend. Are the lines dashed? Swirling? Thick or thin? Colored? You tell me.

POSSIBILITY THREE

the other day, I dreampt of a ring
with two layers. what does it
mean? the diamonds sparkled
in the sun. It was like I knew
the ring, recognized it somehow,
but still where
it was bottom layer
was filled with diamonds all
in a row. The top layer was
non-descript, silver, perhaps
needed to be polished. I
held it I turned it in my
hand, trying to recall where
it came from, who it
belonged to.
EXTEND

YOU THINK: Yep, I'm going to
"extend" my writing all the
way across this page! And
the drawing may intersect
with my words in a cool way?
Let's see what happens. I
SAY: Yes, please. Will you
write from left to right
or from top to bottom?
In a circle? Show me.

POSSIBILITY FOUR

EXTEND

YOU THINK: What's the
prompt? I forgot already. I'm
doing my own thing. I SAY:
Hello, fellow rule breaker!
I'd ask you to post a pic of
your page of wild abandon,
but that will only make you
not want to (I know the
mind of a renegade). Still,
if you use #twujournal
I will smile big time.

WHAT MATERIALS TO USE?

DRAW

In many ways this journal is created with drawing in mind. It is how my brain processes the world. Think of this practice as a meditation on the line. Is the line alive? Yes or no? If no, then what can you do to bring life into the line? Loosening up is usually the best place to start. Physically relax. As you draw, is your hand connected to your eye? Is your eye connected to your heart? Experiment with these sensations. The drawn line is like the breath, always there to tether you to the present moment. Connect to it, summon it to life, and you will be forever changed.

Write

Perhaps you want to fill each nook and crevice of this book with words. Please do. You can write over the images already present and cover the pages with your inner ruminations. Maybe you write a poem inspired by the image or prompt. If there is a quote, mantra, song lyric, or phrase that's particularly meaningful to you right now, try writing it again and again until it's ingrained in your heart (see an example on page 15). If you're up for it, there is something freeing about writing with black ink over a black page. If you don't believe me, try it on the "vent" prompt (pages 130–131). Catharsis awaits. Set the writer in you free.

The possibilities are infinite. Nothing would excite me more than to see you stitching and sewing this book into new shapes, adding fabric, making paper airplane love letters, tie-dyeing the entire journal back to front. That being said, there are four methods that I think are easy access points and some of the most rewarding art practices that I have found. Here's a recap of my favorite ways to use this journal:

paint

If you want more mystery in your life, break out your watercolors and inks. Doodle across the page. Make a complete mess. Have paper towels handy. Be curious about the material—I can't stress this enough. An alchemist (another name for an artist) studies their material. It is their subject. They wonder about the relationship between the pigments, the water, and the air. They throw ideas of "the right way" out the window in search of a deeper and more personal discovery. They are patient and persistent. It is said that watercolor expresses the psyche. Find out if this is true for you. Get curious, loosen up, and see what unfolds.

COLLAGE

Nothing compares to the wonder of collage. Working with it, you will access the imaginative nature of the psyche while bumping up against pop culture. You'll be able to express ideas visually without getting hung up on technique. The critical piece is getting some good source material. I like to gather old magazines, art history books, and nature books from thrift stores. Pick up at least one or two books that are peculiar, mysterious, or not your usual style. For an advanced practice, try picking the books and pages with your eyes closed. I'm serious. Trust the image and let yourself be taken for a ride.

IN RETURN...

Anytime one partakes in a creative journey (as you are doing) they return with a gem, a boon, a realization or skill that was previously out of reach. The pages of this journal are designed to expedite this process of discovery. What follows is a list of potential gems that you may grasp along the way:

STRENGTHEN YOUR SKILLS

This can't be helped. It will happen without you even noticing it! Anytime you hold a pen, paintbrush, or collage materials in your hand and focus the mind you are training yourself to draw, to see, to perceive, to create. This is creative prac- tice !

BE CONNECTED TO US ALL

The whole world walks through the labyrinth. Sometimes we forget this. I am there, you are there, and every artist is there right now. When you work on these pages remember you are connected to everyone else working on these pages, like an intricate mysterious web. Can you feel it ?

CONQUER SELF-LIMITING BELIEFS

If there is a page within this journal that especially frightens you, that is where you will find the gold. Approach it! Delve in! You will quickly find the page cannot do anything to hurt you and is only there to support your practice and growth.

★

EXPAND YOUR MIND

When the mind is puzzled, a wonderful thing happens — it seeks answers in a new and unknown space. This is the essence of creativity. When the mystery arrives, greet it!

BUILD RESILLIENCE

Being frustrated is a necessary part of the creative process. If you do not hit a wall, you have probably not traveled far. Remember the labyrinth? There are many twists and turns. It is tiring at times. Building your capacity to move forward amid frustration is a must for artists. Strengthen the muscle of resilience!

☾

SO... MY FELLOW

YOU HAVE ALREADY
TAKEN
YOUR FIRST STEP.
TO TAKE ANOTHER,

BRAVE TRAVELER...

CLOSE YOUR EYES,
PICK A PAGE...
AND BEGIN.

and remember...

THE WHOLE WORLD

TRAVELS WITH YOU.

EMBELLISH

CONTINUE

DEFINE

ENCIRCLE

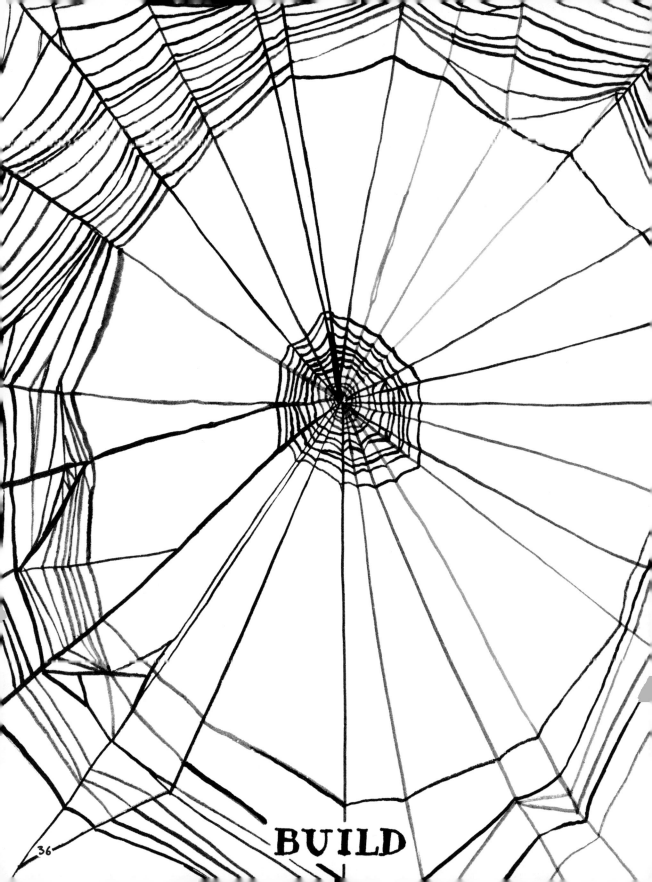

BUILD

ENLARGE

MIRROR

ENVISION

EMANATE

COLOR

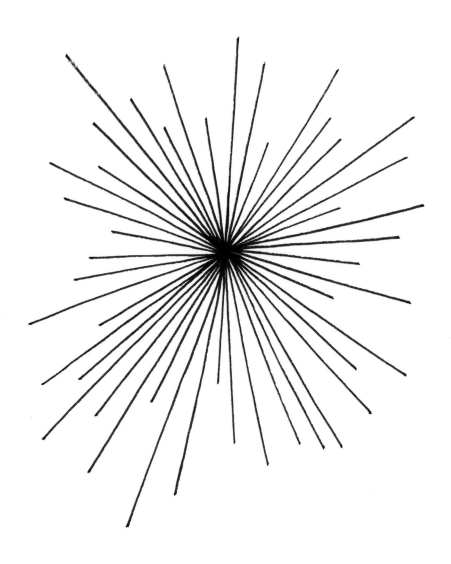

EXTEND

HOLD

CONCEAL

48

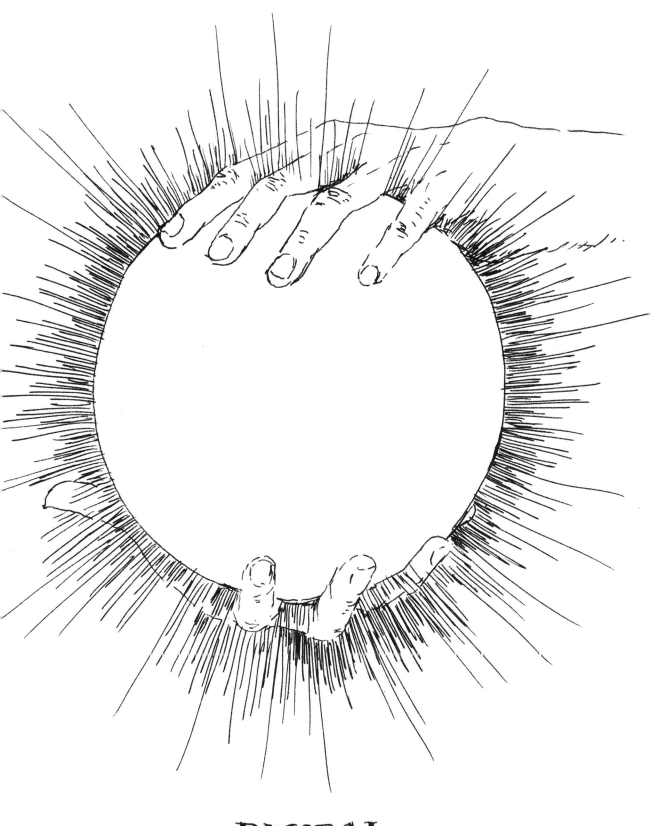

REVEAL

50

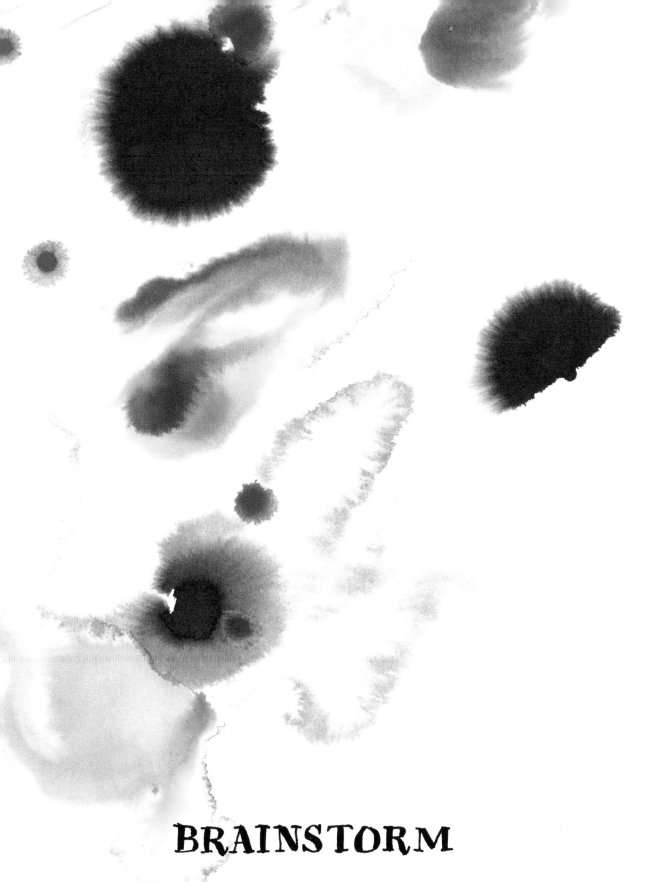

BRAINSTORM

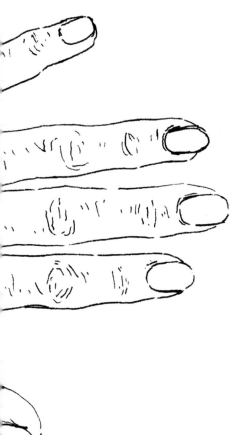

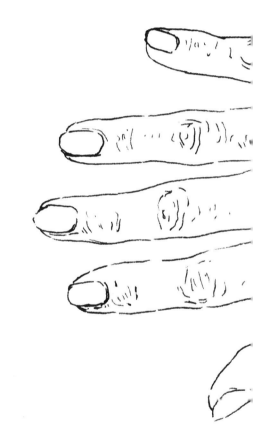

CONNECT

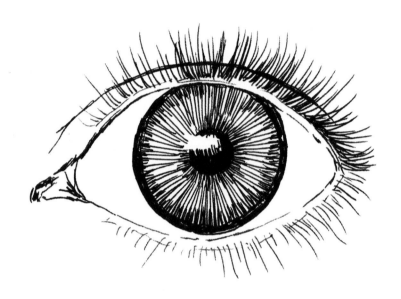

ILLUMINATE

A = △

B = ★

C = ☾

D =

E = 👁

F = ≣

G = ▲

I = ✴

J = ⊘

H = ▼

K = ⊜

L = ►

M = ⛰

N = ▥

O = ≋

P = ⦶

Q = ◑

R = ◐

S = ⚡

T = ⚡

U =

W = ♥

V = ◄

X = ⦿

Z = ☾

Y = ☉

STUDY

DECIPHER

TRANSLATE

58

STRENGTHEN

NARRATE

62

DESTROY

REGENERATE

GRASP

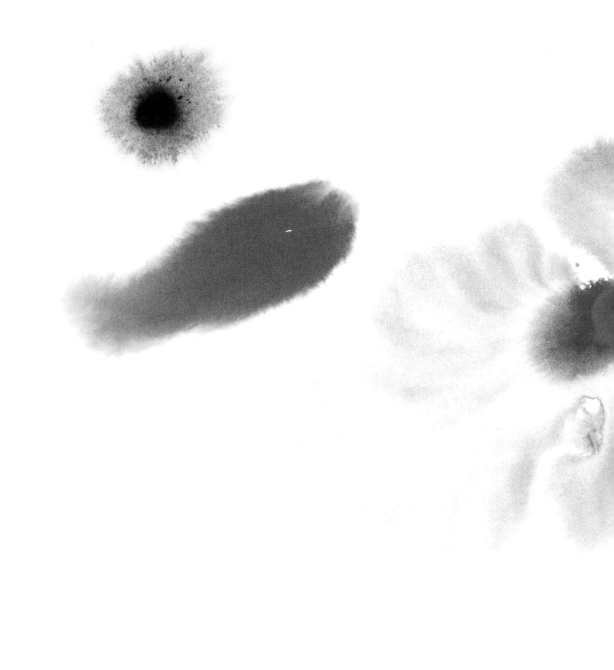

FLIRT

LINK

OBSTRUCT

FEEL

EMULATE

74

DRIFT

ELECTRIFY

MAGNIFY

BLESS

CHERISH

INTENSIFY

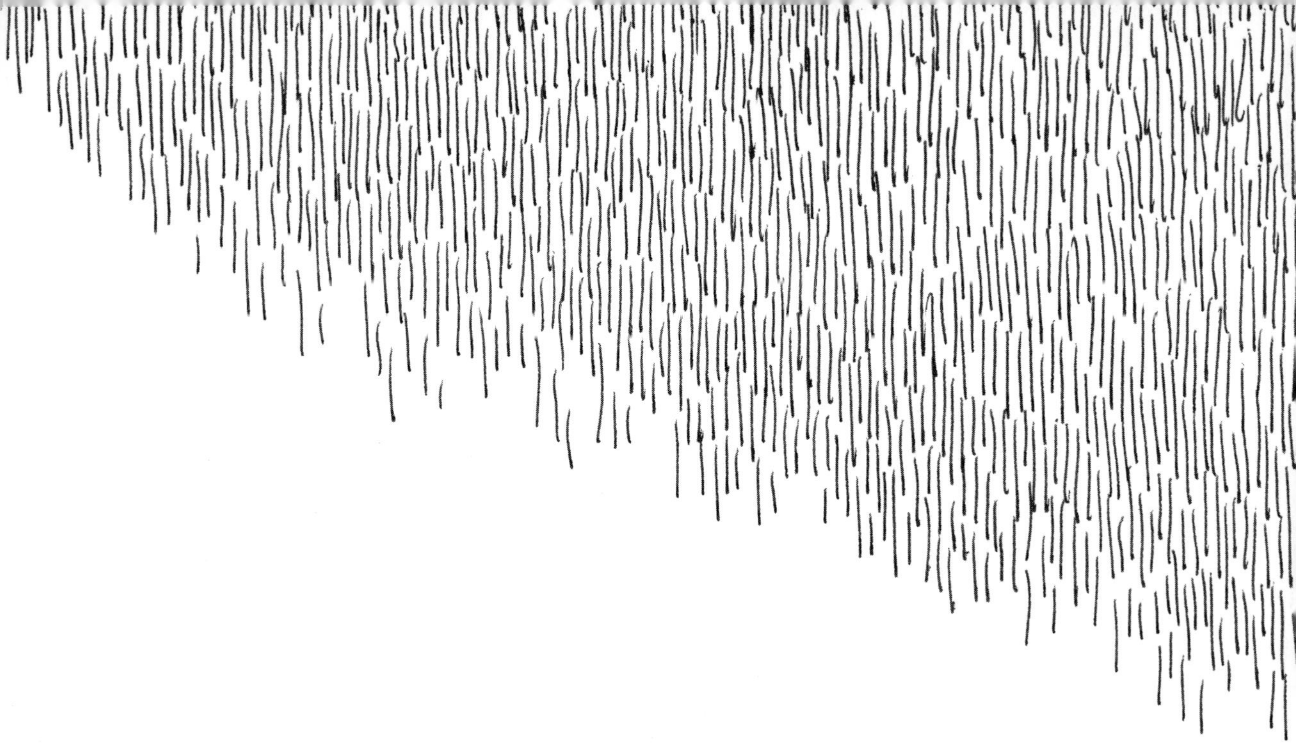

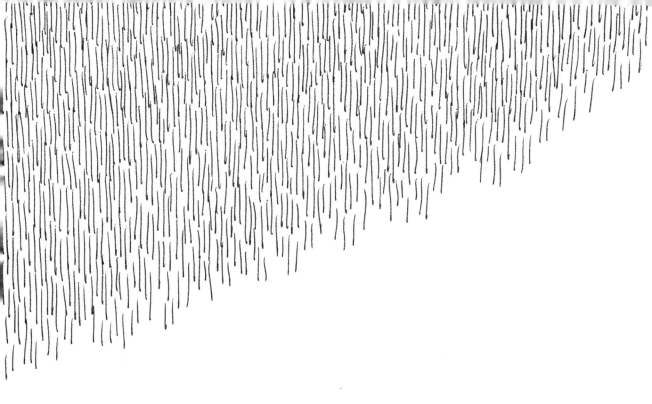

PRACTICE

CHANGE

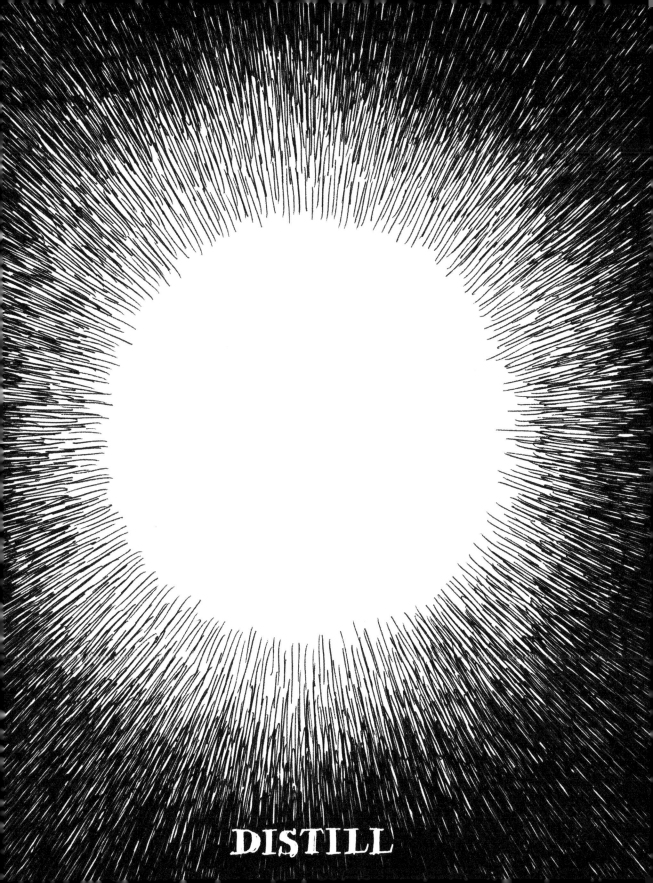

DISTILL

INTERACT

COMPLETE

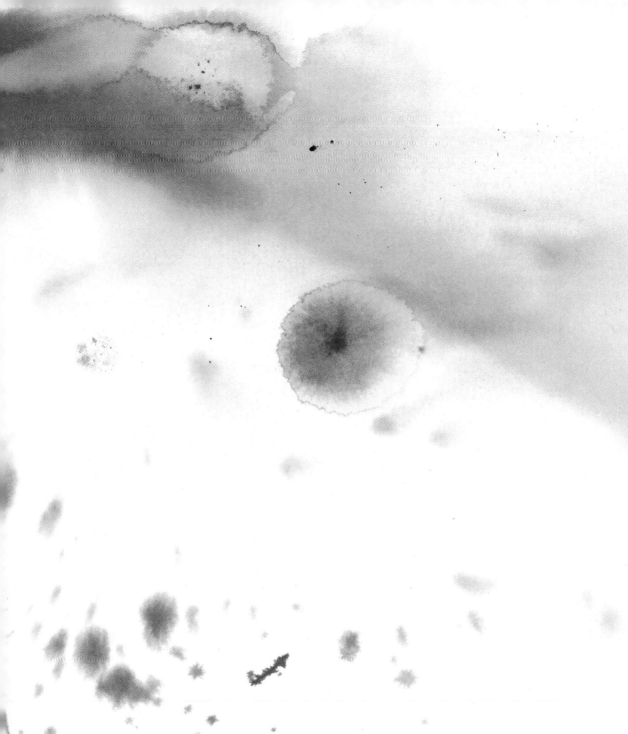

90

GUSH

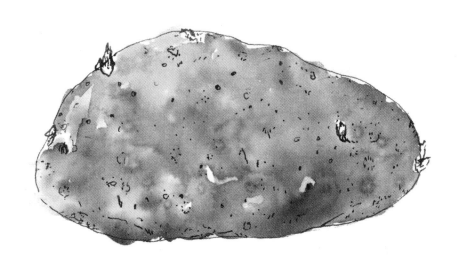

GLORIFY

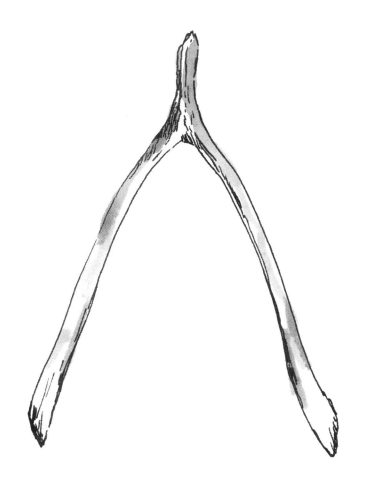

WISH

DECIPHER

TRANSLATE

SURROUND

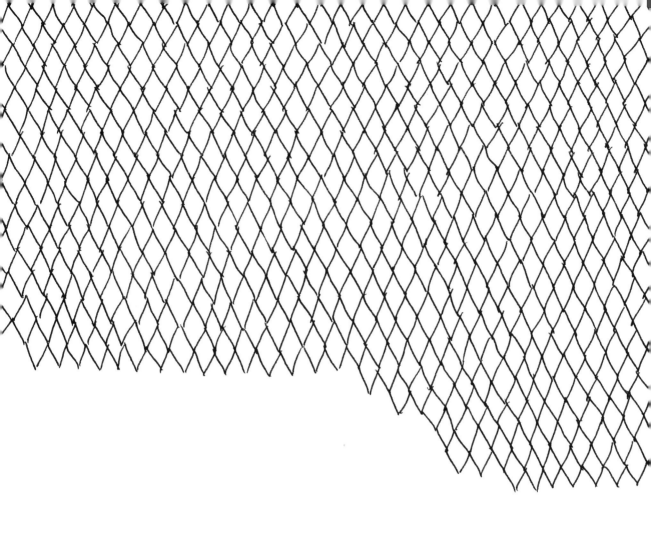

PERSIST

98

ENLIVEN

RUMINATE

MEDITATE

MATCH

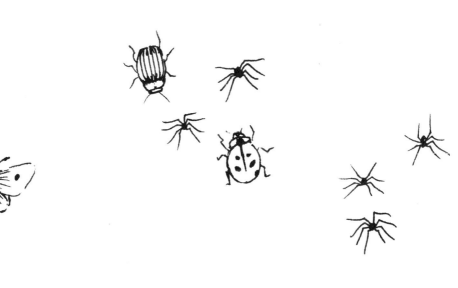

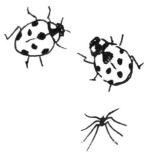

POPULATE

INHABIT

DESCRIBE

108

MEANDER

LISTEN

SPEAK

SIMPLIFY

ELABORATE

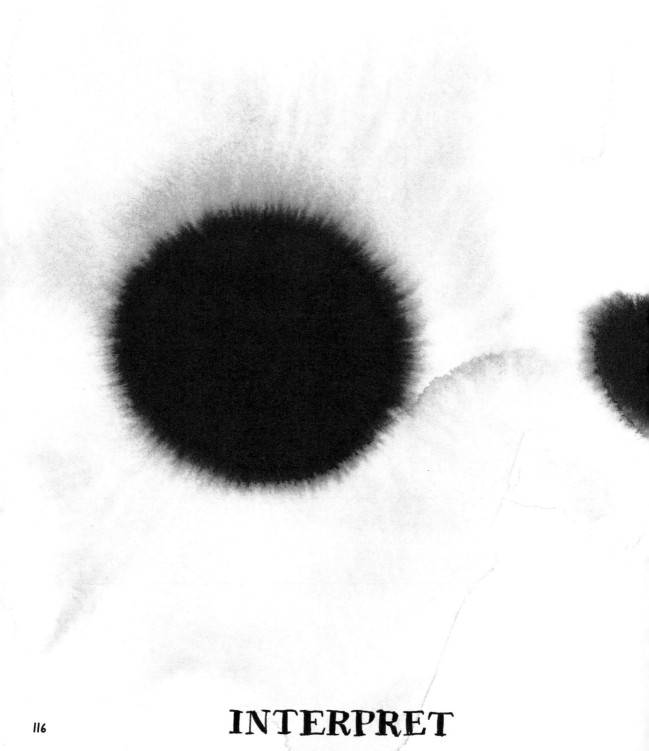

INTERPRET

REMEMBER

UNITE

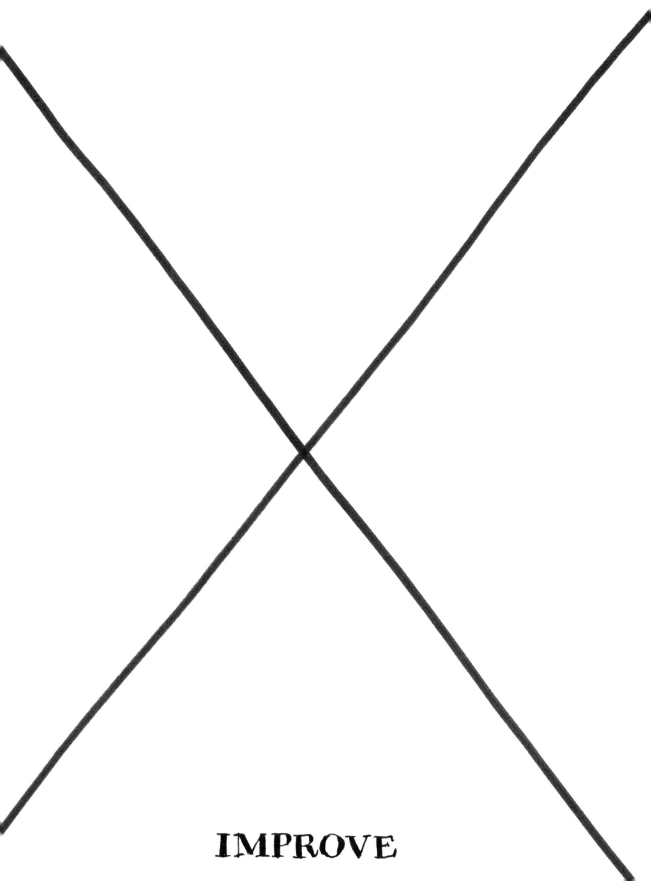

IMPROVE

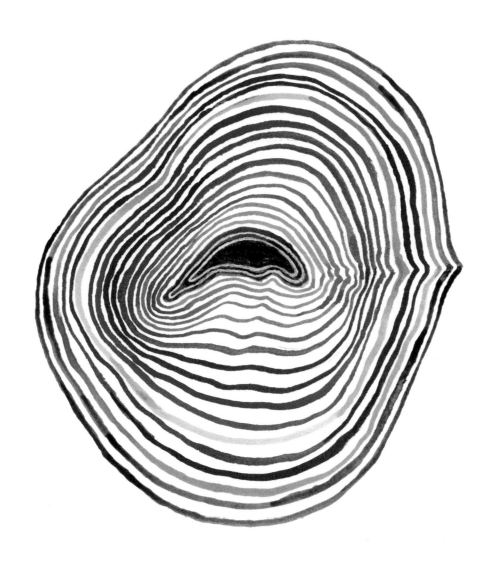

OUTLINE

SATURATE

FILL

IMBUE

DAYDREAM

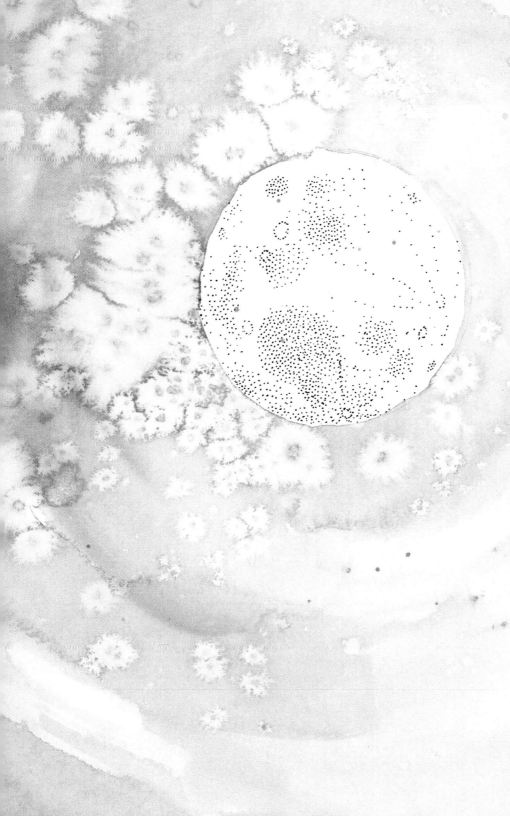

WORSHIP

PROTECT

VENT

AMPLIFY

MULTIPLY

TELL

REPEAT

INITIATE

REPLY

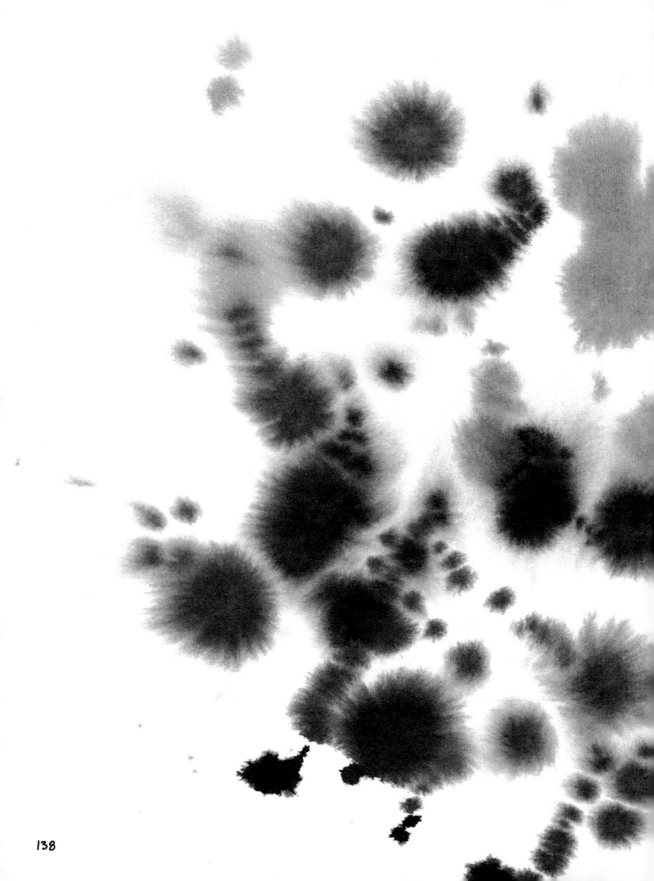

138

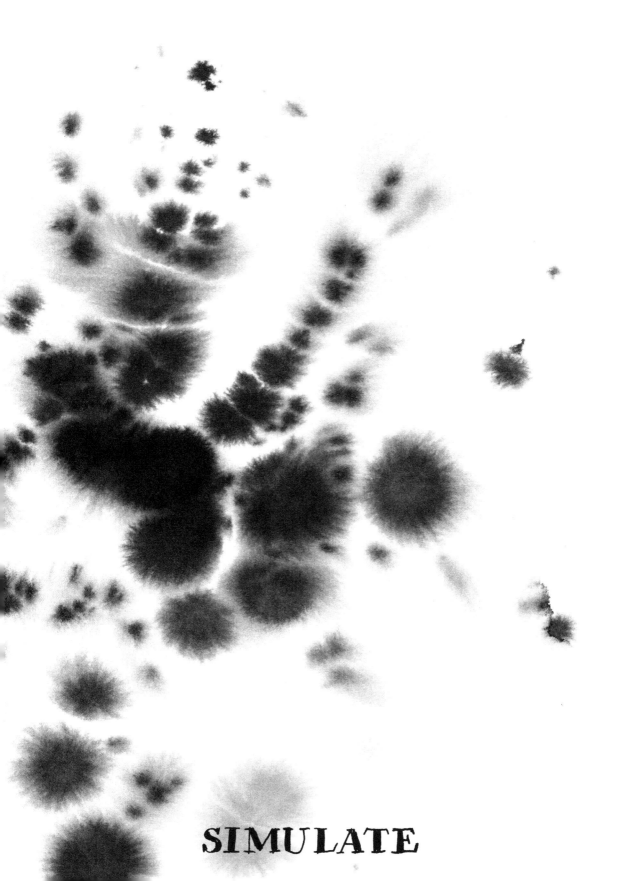

SIMULATE

UPLIFT

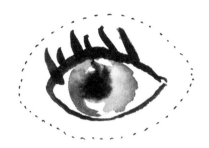

CUT

FRIGHTEN

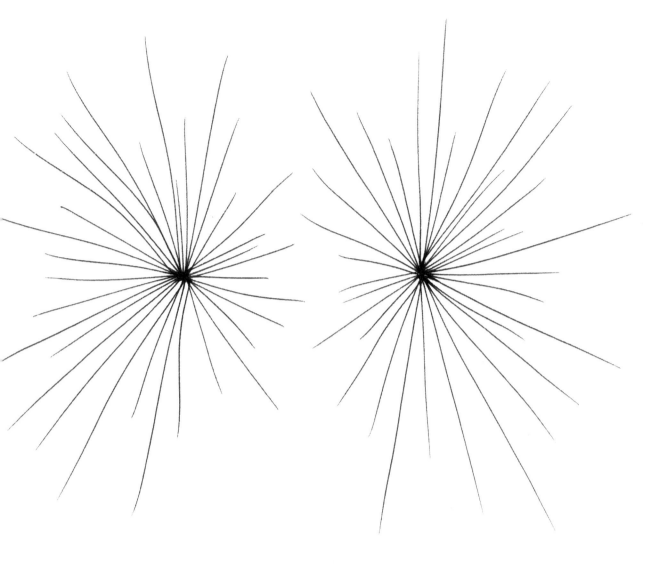

RADIATE

FOCUS

PLAY

DECODE

EXPRESS

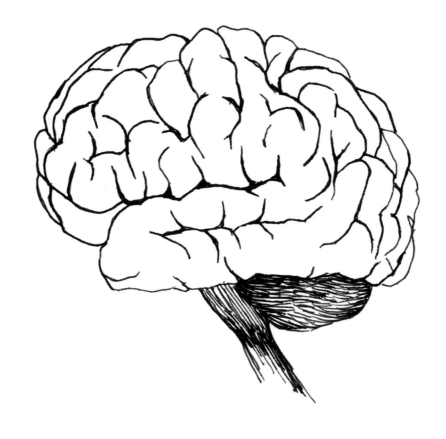

SOOTHE

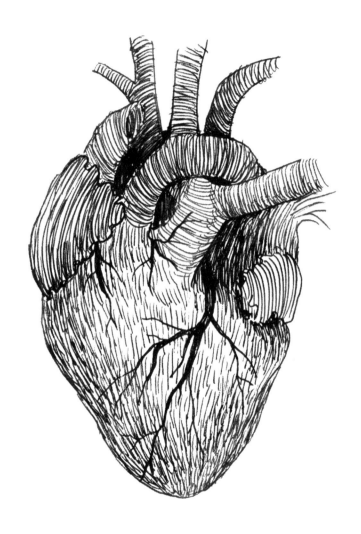

HONOR

A =

B =

C =

D =

E =

F =

G =

H =

I =

J =

K =

L =

M =

N =

O =

P =

Q =

R =

S =

T =

U =

V =

W =

X =

Y =

Z =

INVENT

ENCODE

COMPLICATE

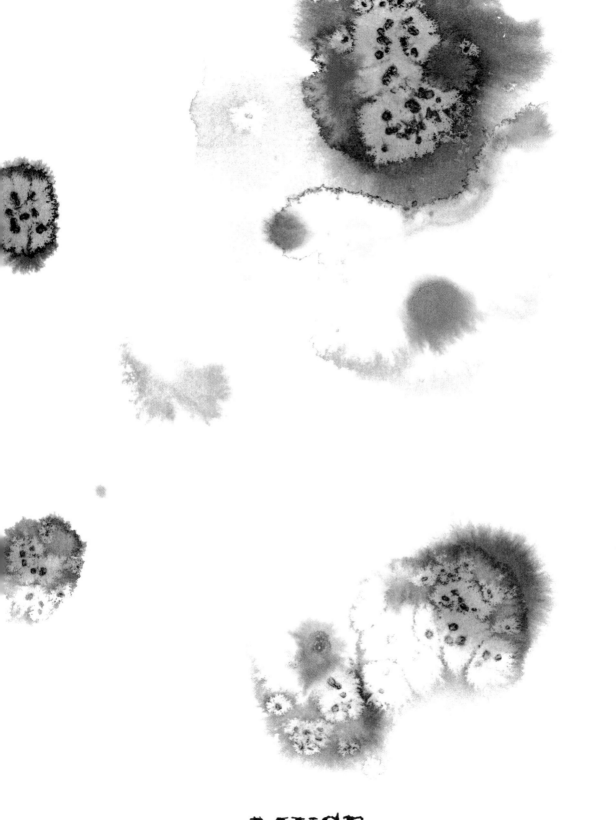

MUSE

154

GRADATE

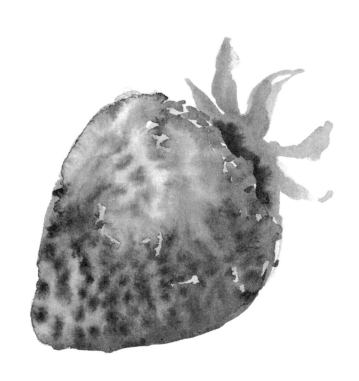

SWEETEN

GROW

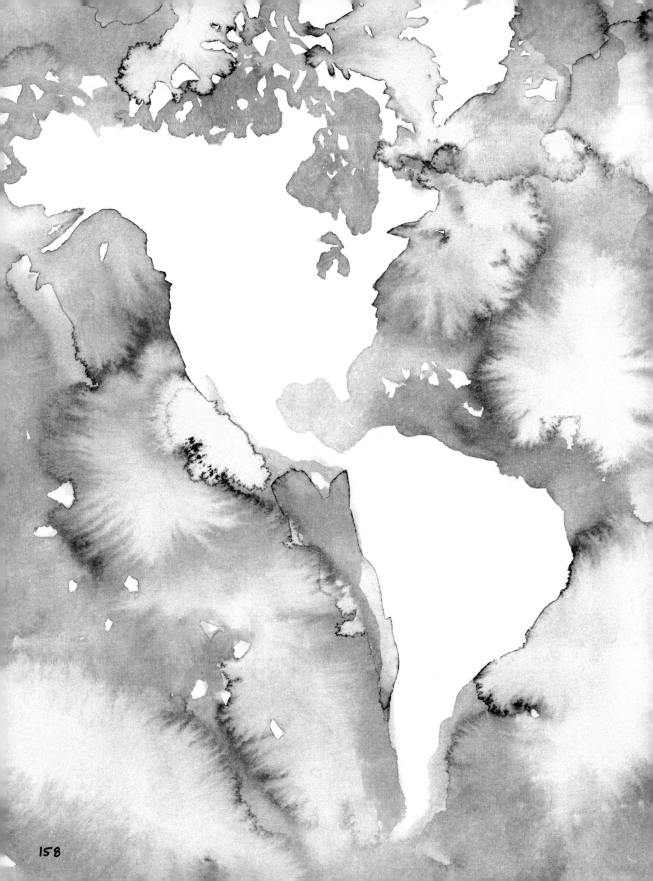

HEAL

EXIT

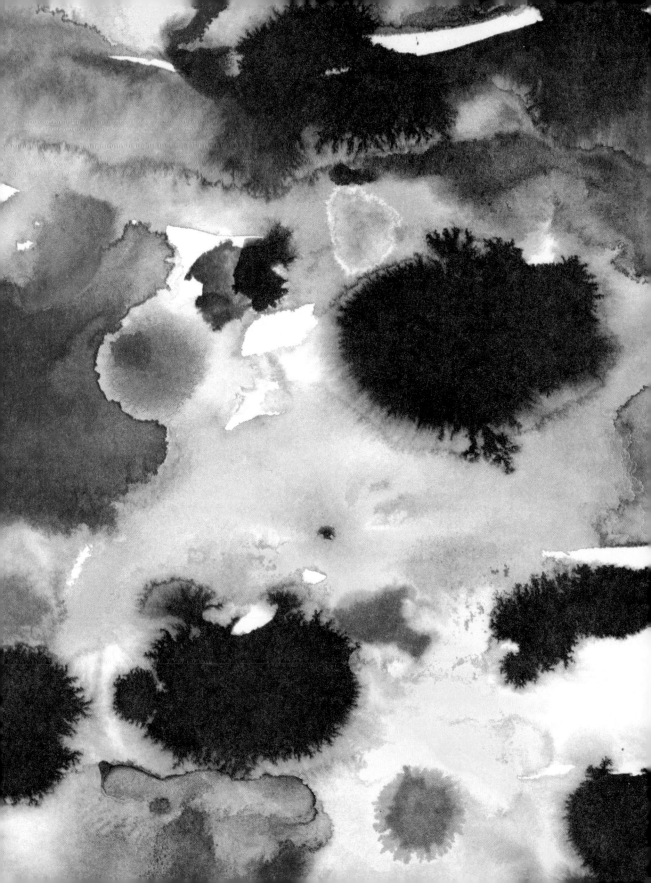